THE PRO FOOTBALL QUIZ BOOK

BY BRUCE WEBER

SCHOLASTIC BOOK SERVICES
New York Toronto London Auckland Sydney Tokyo

To Annette, who richly deserves a solo

Copyright © 1975 by Scholastic Magazines, Inc. All rights
reserved. Published by Scholastic Book Services, a division of Scholastic Magazines, Inc.

1st printing . . . . .November, 1975
Printed in the U.S.A.

CONTENTS

Double Teaming 1

Up From the Colleges 19

Today's Superstars—and Yesterday's 27

Whistles and Flags 45

All Over the Field 51

The Big Games 72

The national pastime? Sure we'll get arguments. But here's one vote for pro football.

Every Sunday—and Monday night—from September through January, the pros of the NFL capture most of the nation's attention. The camera eyes of all three major networks, the voices of the leading sportscasters, and typewriters of hundreds of sportswriters all focus on the action.

All this coverage has created a nation of experts. Everyone knows pro football. Everyone knows the names, the places, the facts, the figures.

Are you an expert? You'll find out in the next 90 or so pages. Some of the questions are hard; some are relatively easy. In any event, you should have fun trying to come up with the answers. Enjoy!

—Bruce Weber

DOUBLE TEAMING

The Team's the Thing!

1. Which team has won the most NFL championships?

    The Green Bay Packers have won the crown 11 times. Only the Chicago Bears, with eight, are close. No other team has won more than four titles.

2. When Oakland defeated Miami in 1973, the Dolphins' 18-game regular and post-season game win streak ended. Whose record did the Dolphins tie?

    The Chicago Bears. The Bears did it twice, in 1933-34 and 1941-42.

3. Which team led its conference the most consecutive seasons?

    The Cleveland Browns. Coach Paul Brown's team took its conference title from 1950, its first year in the NFL, through 1955, a record six straight years.

4. The all-time pro record for points in a season was set by an AFL team. Which one?

    The 1961 Houston Oilers. Led by quarterback George Blanda, the Oilers scored 513 points in 14 games, an average of 36.6 per game.

5. An NFL team once gained 735 yards in one game. Which one?

The Los Angeles Rams did it against the New York Yanks in 1951, the Yanks' last year in the league.

6. Which team gained the fewest yards in a game?

Gained is the wrong word. The Denver Broncos' total yardage against the Raiders on Sept. 10, 1967, was *minus* five yards. Denver's problems enabled Oakland's Roger Bird to set a record by returning nine punts.

7. The passingest team in pro history? The 1964 Houston Oilers. How many times did they throw?

592, with George Blanda accounting for 505 of them.

8. Fans of the running game loved the Cardinals-Lions game in 1935. The two teams attempted only four passes. How many were completed?

One, by Detroit. The record was tied by the Lions and Cleveland Rams in 1937.

9. What's the record for pass completions in a season?

301, by the 1967 Washington Redskins.

10. The 1961 Houston Oilers traveled by air. How many passing yards did they gain?

4,392, just eight yards short of $2\frac{1}{2}$ miles.

11. Which team's quarterbacks were sacked the most times in a season?

Atlanta's, 70 times in 1968, including 11 in one game against St. Louis. Pittsburgh's quarterbacks had the worst single day. They were sacked 12 times against Dallas in 1966.

12. Which team threw for the most touchdowns in a season?

The pass-crazy 1961 Oilers. They connected on 48 TD strikes, 36 by George Blanda.

13. What's the NFL record for the most punts in a single game?

17, by the Bears and Cincinnati. Oddly, the teams set the record on the same day, Oct 22, 1933. The Bears punted 17 times against the Packers, and Cincinnati 17 times against Pittsburgh.

14. The Bears also hold the record for fewest punts in a season. How many?

32, in their championship season of 1941.

15. The 1970 Los Angeles Rams returned 62 punts, one better than the old NFL record. But they didn't even lead the league. Which team beat the Rams and set a new standard?

The Denver Broncos with 63.

16. Which team set the record for most fair catches in a season?

The 1971 Baltimore Colts—34. The 1961 Cowboys and 1967 Jets share the record for the fewest, with three.

17. The New England Patriots have played in several stadiums throughout the Boston area. But they played one home game outside of New England. Where?

Legion Field in Birmingham, Ala. A stadium conflict with the baseball Red Sox forced them out of Fenway Park. They went to Birmingham where Jet quarterback Joe Namath helped them draw a fine crowd.

18. Until 1956, when they moved to Yankee Stadium, where did the New York Giants play?

   The Polo Grounds.

19. Until 1964 (when they moved to Shea Stadium), where did the New York Titans-Jets play their home games?

   Once again, the Polo Grounds.

20. The Lions and Cardinals (along with the Titans) share the pro record for TD punt returns in one game with two. What's so unusual about their record?

   Each team did it *twice* — during the same season! Detroit turned the double-TD trick against Los Angeles and Green Bay in 1951. The Chicago Cardinals double-whammied the Steelers and the Giants in 1959.

21. Of the eight original AFL teams, how many are playing in their original stadiums?

   Only one. Denver is still at Mile High Stadium where they started in 1960.

22. Which team returned the most kickoffs in one season?

   The Atlanta Falcons brought back 82 kickoffs in 1966, their first NFL season.

23. The Cleveland Browns set a record by fumbling only eight times during the 1959 season. Which team holds the record for most fumbles?

The 1938 Chicago Bears coughed the ball up 56 times during an 11-game season. Despite their slippery fingers, the Bears still won six and lost only five games.

24. What is the pro record for opponents' fumbles recovered in a season?

31, by the Minnesota Vikings in 1963.

25. The cleanest team in pro history was penalized only 19 times for 139 yards — for an entire season! Which team was it?

The 1937 Detroit Lions.

26. What is the record for most penalty yardage in one game?

209 yards on 21 penalties by the Cleveland Browns in 1951. Their opponents, the Chicago Bears, were penalized 165 yards and their combined total of 374 yards established a two-team penalty mark.

27. The 1966 New York Giants' defense had more holes than Swiss cheese. How many points did they allow?

501, including a record 66 touchdowns!

28. Which stingy club allowed the fewest points in one season?

The 1932 Chicago Bears. George Halas' defenders gave up 44 points in 14 games, an average of just over three per game. Interestingly, the Bears won only seven games but still won the NFL championship over Green Bay's 10-game winners.

6

The reason? Chicago had six ties (a 7-1-6 record). With ties not counted at that time, Chicago's 7-1 record produced a better percentage than Green Bay's 10-3.

29. For years, the Bears were always the defensive leaders. The 1942 team allowed the fewest rushing yards in a season. How many?

519 in 11 games, a little more than 47 yards per game.

30. The Lions, Cowboys, and Vikings share a most impressive defensive record. Which one?

Fewest rushing touchdowns allowed in a season — two. Dallas (1968) and Minnesota (1971) did it in 14 games; Detroit (1934) played only 13 games.

31. Which AFC team holds the NFL record for most interceptions in a season? (Hint: They set it back in AFL days.)

The 1961 San Diego Chargers with 49, an average of 3½ in each of their 14 games.

32. Which team returned intercepted passes for the most yardage?

Again, it's the 1961 Chargers. They returned those 49 interceptions for 929 yards, an average of nearly 18 yards per return. The 929 yards are more than 200 yards better than the all-time second-best mark, 712 yards by the 1952 L. A. Rams.

33. Which team returned intercepted passes for the most touchdowns in one season?

Now you've got the idea. Sure, it's the 1961 Chargers with nine. No other team ever had more than six!

7

34. One of the biggest changes in pro football has been the importance of the special teams. They're responsible for kickoffs, punts, and place kicks. Which "special" team allowed the most yards per kickoff over a season?

The 1972 New York Jets gave up 29.5 yards per kick.

35. Which team gained the most average yards on kickoffs during a season?

1972 must've been a good year. The '72 Bears gained 29.4 yards per kickoff.

36. The 1948 Bears hold the record for most yards returning punts. How many?

781. The second-best 1950 Green Bay Packers gained 729 yards.

37. The 1969 Oakland Raiders closed the old AFL by setting an all-time pro record they're not proud of. Which one?

Most yards penalized. The yellow flags cost the Raiders 1,274 yards in 14 games.

38. Until 1940, what was the penalty for clipping?

25 yards.

39. What was the first pro team to train away from its home town?

The 1929 Chicago Cardinals, who held their pre-season workouts in Coldwater, Mich.

40. Who won the first AFL game ever played?

The Denver Broncos. They defeated the Boston Patriots, 13-10, on Sept. 9, 1960.

41. The worst team in pro history? Probably the Chicago Cardinals. They went from mid-1942 to mid-1945 without a victory. How many did they lose?

29 straight, including 0-10 seasons in 1943 and '44 — when they were combined with the Pittsburgh Steelers.

42. When the Giants visited the Lions on Nov. 7, 1943, the offensive units must've stayed home. The teams played a 0-0 tie. What was the importance of that game?

It was the last 0-0 tie in NFL play. Though 15 previous games ended scoreless, no two teams in the next 30-plus years have been able to match the record.

43. Two AFL teams drove the scoreboard operator crazy back in 1963. In the second quarter of a game, the Houston Oilers scored 21 points. But they lost ground to their opponents who scored 28. Name this high-powered team, coached in that game by Al Davis.

The Oakland Raiders. The combined 49 points set a two-team NFL record. Incidentally, Oakland won 52-49 in the second-highest scoring NFL game ever.

Where Do They Play?

1. Buffalo Bills
2. Dallas Cowboys
3. Minnesota Vikings
4. Cincinnati Bengals
5. Kansas City Chiefs
6. San Francisco 49ers
7. Washington Redskins
8. New York Jets
9. Cleveland Browns
10. Denver Broncos
11. Chicago Bears
12. Philadelphia Eagles
13. Green Bay Packers
14. New England Patriots
15. Miami Dolphins
16. Oakland Raiders
17. St. Louis Cardinals
18. Pittsburgh Steelers
19. Los Angeles Rams
20. Houston Oilers

a. Shea Stadium
b. Candlestick Park
c. Soldier Field
d. Memorial Coliseum
e. Schaefer Stadium
f. Alameda County Coliseum
g. Busch Memorial Stadium
h. Riverfront Stadium
i. Veterans Stadium
j. Municipal Stadium
k. Three Rivers Stadium
l. Rich Stadium
m. Orange Bowl
n. Arrowhead
o. R. R. Kennedy Stadium
p. Texas Stadium
q. Astrodome
r. Lambeau Field
s. Metropolitan Stadium
t. Mile High Stadium

1:l; 2:p; 3:s; 4:h; 5:n; 6:b; 7:o; 8:a; 9:j; 10:t; 11:c; 12:i; 13:r; 14:e; 15:m; 16:f; 17:g; 18:k; 19:d; 20:q.

Remember the AFL?

1. Who was the first commissioner of the American Football League?

   Joe Foss, former governor of South Dakota and World War II flying ace. He served from 1960 through April 7, 1966.

2. Who succeeded Foss as AFL commissioner?

   Al Davis, general manager and coach of the Oakland Raiders.

3. Which player jumped from the AFL to the NFL, thereby prompting the merger of the leagues?

   Kicker Pete Gogolak of the Buffalo Bills who joined the New York Giants.

4. Which two teams played in the first exhibition game between the AFL and NFL?

   The Denver Broncos (AFL) and the Detroit Lions (NFL). Denver won.

5. What do Ger Schwedes, Richie Lucas, Don Meredith, Roger LeClerc, Billy Cannon, Monty Stickles, Dale Hackbart, and George Izo have in common?

   They were the first players selected in the first-ever AFL college draft.

6. How many rounds were included in the first AFL draft?

   An unbelievable 53! The eight teams selected 33 players each on Nov. 22, 1959, and an additional 20 on Dec. 2, 1959.

7. Which team won the first AFL championship?

The Houston Oilers, led by quarterback George Blanda, defeated the Los Angeles Chargers, 24-16 on Jan. 1, 1961, for the first AFL title.

8. When the president of the hapless New York Titans announced a home crowd of 18,000 at the Polo Grounds, a sportswriter commented that 17,000 came disguised as empty seats. Who was the president of the Titans?

Harry Wismer, nationally famous as a sportscaster.

9. When the Titans went broke, who bought the team and renamed it Jets?

A group headed by David (Sonny) Werblin.

10. Which teams played in the second AFL championship game?

The same teams that played the first time, the Oilers and Chargers. One difference: the Chargers had moved from Los Angeles to San Diego. But some things never change: the Oilers won again, 10-3.

11. The third AFL championship game was, to that point, the longest game in pro history. Who won it?

The Dallas Texans. A 25-yard field goal by Tommy Brooker after 77 minutes, 54 seconds gave Dallas a 20-17 victory over Houston's defending champions. Dallas' glory was short-lived. Little more than a month later, owner Lamar Hunt moved the team to Kansas City and changed its nickname to Chiefs.

12. Who was the first coach of the Boston Patriots?

Lou Saban, who has also coached the Buffalo Bills and Denver Broncos in the AFL and AFC.

13. When the AFL was born, what change did they make in the scoring rules?

They adopted the college two-point conversion rule. Two points were awarded for running or passing the ball over the goal line.

14. What all-time great Redskin quarterback was the first coach of the New York Titans?

Slingin' Sammy Baugh.

15. What year did the Jets move from the Polo Grounds to Shea Stadium?

1964.

16. Where did the Boston Patriots play for the first three years of the AFL?

Boston University Field.

17. Who was the Dallas Texans' first coach?

Hank Stram. He stayed with the club in Dallas and Kansas City until he was fired after the 1974 season.

18. Which network televised AFL games for its first five years?

The American Broadcasting Company (ABC).

19. Which two teams played in the AFL's first divisional playoff game?

The Boston Patriots and Buffalo Bills. Boston won 26-8 on December 28, 1963. The Pats went on to lose to San Diego 51-10 in the championship game.

20. Who was the Chargers' first coach?
Sid Gillman.

21. Al Davis was the AFL's last commissioner. Who led the league as president after the merger agreement?
Milt Woodard.

22. The AFL remained an eight-club league until 1966 when it added its ninth team. Which one?
The Miami Dolphins.

23. The AFL's tenth team entered the league in 1968. Which one was it?
The Cincinnati Bengals.

24. Who was the Oakland Raiders' first coach?
Eddie Erdelatz, who had enjoyed great success at the Naval Academy.

Suburban Living

Like many businesses, football teams are moving to the suburbs. NFL clubs are playing in cities called Irving, Foxboro, and Bloomington. Match the clubs with their *real* home cities

1. Orchard Park
2. Bloomington
3. Foxboro
4. Irving
5. Flushing

a. Dallas Cowboys
b. New York Jets
c. Buffalo Bills
d. Minnesota Vikings
e. New England Patriots

1:c; 2:d; 3:e; 4:a; 5:b.

Two other teams are also moving to the suburbs; their new stadiums are in Pontiac and Hackensack. Which teams will play there?

The Lions' new home is in Pontiac, Mich.; the Giants' new ballpark will be in Hackensack, N. J.

Good Old Days

All of the following cities were once represented in the National Football League. Match
the city with its team nickname:

1.	Hammond (Ind.)	a.	Jeffersons
2.	Dayton (Ohio)	b.	Panhandles
3.	Rochester (N.Y.)	c.	Yellow Jackets
4.	Canton (Ohio)	d.	Maroons
5.	Decatur (Ill.)	e.	Spartans
6.	Frankford (Pa.)	f.	Pros
7.	Akron (Ohio)	g.	Steamrollers
8.	Brooklyn (N.Y.)	h.	Bulldogs
9.	Muncie (Ind.)	i.	Tigers
10.	Columbus (Ohio)	j.	Steels
11.	Toledo (Ohio)	k.	Triangles
12.	Duluth (Minn.)	l.	Stapletons
13.	Providence (R.I.)	m.	Eskimos
14.	Staten Island (N.Y.)	n.	Dodgers
15.	Portsmouth (Ohio)	o.	Staleys

1:f; 2:k; 3:a; 4:h; 5:o; 6:c; 7:j; 8:n; 9:i; 10:b; 11:d;
    12:m; 13:g; 14:l; 15:e.

Hidden Cities--NFL Style

We've taken the 25 NFL locations (New York has two teams) and buried them in a maze of letters. Some of them read right to left, others left to right, some are top to bottom, still others read bottom to top. When you find one, circle it—as we've done in the example below. By the way, the answers are on the next page.

```
H P E D L R M U L O S A N G E L E S M I
Z D A G G R E E N B A Y Q U I B N O I P
L I L T A G I F T R L C A G E V E I N Z
P I O U T H A V S T L O U I S X W B N T
T I L E A G E R L M A N A G Y P E C E S
A T H B E R E V N E D N P Z W Q N T S A
P I T R A U N M C P W A S H I N G T O N
N T S A M B U F F A L O I P L U L U T F
H A T T I S A G F T E M P O L E A K A R
E N I K A T Y R E A S O V H U T N E R A
N N O A A T L A N T A R P L E X D O B N
E I R N T I O M A H N H O U S T O N A C
W C G S O P H I L A D E L P H I A U L I
O N I A K D E T R O I T V Z A B K I T S
R I M S O N E S I X E A B S P O L T I C
L C A C H I C A G O G E A T A Z A Q M O
E R M I A M I J E B O S W A M T N I O Z
A U P T U N C K C L E V E L A N D U R A
N E W Y O R K E X P E N T S I O W H E N
S A G E R S I C I A D S T P A T R O K E
```

Hidden Cities--Discovered

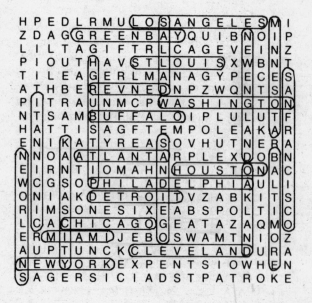

```
H P E D L R M U L O S A N G E L E S M I
Z D A G G R E E N B A Y Q U I B N O I P Z
L I L T A G I F T R L C A G E V E I N Z T
P I O U T H A V S T L O U I S X W B C T S A
T I L E A G E R L M A N A G Y P E C T E N
A T H B E R E V N E D N P Z W Q N T E S A
P N I T R A U N M C P W A S H I N G T O N
N A S A M B U F F A L O I P L U L U T F
H T I I S A G F T E M P O L E A K A R
E N O K A T Y R E A S O V H U T N E B A
N I G A T L A N T A R P L E X D O R N
W C R A N T I O M A H N H O U S T O N B A C
O I I N S O P H I L A D E L P H I A U L I T
R N M S A K D E T R O I T V Z A B K I T C
L C A S O N E S I X E A B S P O L T M O
E A C H I C A G O G E A T A Z A Q I Z
A R M I A M I J E B O S W A M T N I O A
U P T U N C K C L E V E L A N D U R A
N E W Y O R K E X P E N T S I O W H E N
S A G E R S I C I A D S T P A T R O K E
```

UP FROM THE COLLEGES

Caught in the Draft

Possibly the greatest honor that a college player can receive is being selected first in the NFL draft. Identify the following first draft choices:

1. The former Notre Dame defensive end, selected first by Buffalo in 1972.

2. The Tennessee State defensive end, selected first by Dallas in 1974.

3. The Louisiana Tech quarterback, selected first by Pittsburgh in 1970.

4. The Michigan State defensive tackle, now with Oakland, selected first by Baltimore in 1967.

5. The Stanford quarterback, selected first by New England in 1971.

6. The Southern Cal running back, selected first by Buffalo in 1969.

7. The Tampa defensive end, now with Kansas City, selected first by Houston in 1973.

8. The Southern Cal tackle, selected first by Minnesota in 1968.

9. The California quarterback, selected first by Atlanta in 1975.

10. The Texas linebacker, selected first by Atlanta in 1966.

1. Walt Patulski; 2. Ed "Too Tall" Jones; 3. Terry Bradshaw; 4. Bubba Smith; 5. Jim Plunkett; 6. O. J. Simpson; 7. John Matuszak; 8. Ron Yary; 9. Steve Bartkowski; 10. Tommy Nobis.

The Heisman Trophy

No Heisman Trophy winner has ever made the
Pro Hall of Fame. (O. J. Simpson may become
the first.) Yet some have excelled in the pros.
Match the Heisman Trophy winners with their
colleges:

1.	John Cappelletti	a.	Southern Cal
2.	Jim Plunkett	b.	Auburn
3.	Steve Spurrier	c.	Penn State
4.	O. J. Simpson	d.	Oklahoma
5.	Roger Staubach	e.	Stanford
6.	Paul Hornung	f.	Navy
7.	Steve Owens	g.	Florida
8.	Pat Sullivan	h.	Notre Dame

1:c; 2:e; 3:g; 4:a; 5:f; 6:h; 7:d; 8:b.

The Outland Trophy

The Football Writers Association awards the Outland Trophy to the nation's number-one college lineman every year. Most become top pros. Match the Outland Trophy winners with their colleges.

1.	Mike Reid	a.	Texas
2.	Merlin Olsen	b.	Southern Cal
3.	John Hicks	c.	Penn State
4.	Randy White	d.	Minnesota
5.	Ron Yary	e.	Utah State
6.	Bobby Bell	f.	Ohio State
7.	Bill Stanfill	g.	Maryland
8.	Tommy Nobis	h.	Georgia

1:c; 2:e; 3:f; 4:g; 5:b; 6:d; 7:h; 8:a.

One of a Kind

Notre Dame, Southern Cal, Ohio State, Purdue, Michigan State — all these schools have turned out more than 100 NFL players. Some schools, however, have produced just *one* in more than 40 years — until 1975. Identify these pros from the following descriptions:

1. Kansas City's giant defensive lineman from William Penn College.

   Wilbur Young.

2. The Chargers' 6-6, 255-pound tackle from Jacksonville State.

   Terry Owens.

3. The former Colt and 49er receiver from the College of Idaho. Hint: He invented the Alley-Oop pass.

   R. C. Owens.

4. The Giants' all-pro tight end from Bloomsburg State.

   Bob Tucker.

5. The U. of Nebraska coach and former Redskin end who graduated from Hastings College.

   Tom Osborne.

6. The former Packer running back who attended Philander Smith.

   Elijah Pitts.

7. No Juniata graduate has ever played in the NFL. One, however, became a head coach with the Rams. Name him.

Chuck Knox.

8. The Falcon linebacker who attended the University of Nevada, Las Vegas.

Ken Mitchell.

9. Though Alex Karras says he attended the University of Mars, there is an Oakland defensive tackle who didn't go to college. Who is he?

Otis Sistrunk.

10. What do the following pros have in common: Garo Yepremian, Mirro Roder, Herb Mul-Key, Horst Muhlmann, John Leypoldt, and Bobby Howfield.

Like Sistrunk, they didn't attend college.

College Men

Match the NFL coaches with the colleges they served as head coach:

1. Lou Saban
2. Paul Brown
3. John Ralston
4. Chuck Fairbanks
5. Tommy Prothro
6. Rick Forzano
7. Don Coryell
8. George Allen

a. Navy
b. Whittier
c. Maryland
d. San Diego State
e. Oklahoma
f. Stanford
g. Ohio State
h. UCLA

1:c; 2:g; 3:f; 4:e; 5:h; 6:a; 7:d; 8:b.

Academic Arms

Match these pro quarterbacks with the colleges they attended:

1.	Ken Anderson	a.	New Mexico State
2.	George Blanda	b.	Columbia
3.	Terry Bradshaw	c.	Florida
4.	Marty Domres	d.	Stanford
5.	Joe Ferguson	e.	Augustana
6.	Roman Gabriel	f.	Mississippi
7.	Joe Gilliam	g.	Georgia
8.	John Hadl	h.	Massachusetts
9.	Bob Griese	i.	Louisiana Tech
10.	Charley Johnson	j.	Kentucky
11.	Sonny Jurgensen	k.	Arkansas
12.	Bill Kilmer	l.	Alabama
13.	Greg Landry	m.	Purdue
14.	Archie Manning	n.	UCLA
15.	Craig Morton	o.	Tennessee State
16.	Joe Namath	p.	Santa Clara
17.	Dan Pastorini	q.	North Carolina St.
18.	Jim Plunkett	r.	Kansas
19.	Steve Spurrier	s.	Duke
20.	Fran Tarkenton	t.	California

1:e; 2:j; 3:i; 4:b; 5:k; 6:q; 7:o; 8:r; 9:m; 10:a; 11:s; 12:n; 13:h; 14:f; 15:t; 16:l; 17:p; 18:d; 19:c; 20:g.

TODAY'S SUPERSTARS— AND YESTERDAY'S

Future Hall Of Famers

To many, Canton, Ohio, means the Professional Football Hall of Fame. Nearly 90 members have already been enshrined. But there's plenty of room for more. Like these stars of today who'll be represented in Canton sometime soon:

O. J. Simpson

1. What do the initials O. J. stand for?

    Orenthal James or, as the fans prefer, Orange Juice.

2. What college did O. J. attend?

    Southern Cal.

3. The greatest rushing season ever? That was 1973 for O. J. How many yards did he gain?

    2,003. Second-best? Jim Brown with 1,803.

4. Simpson set the record for most carries in a game on a Monday night against Kansas City. How many times did he run?

    39. That helped him set a season record with 332 carries.

5. During his record rushing season, how many times did O. J. rush for over 100 yards?

    11.

Joe Namath

1. Though he played college ball at Alabama, Namath made his Beaver Falls High School team famous, too. In what state is Beaver Falls located?

   Pennsylvania.

2. When Joe graduated from Alabama, the Jets' owner gave him more than $400,000 to sign with New York. Who was the Jets' famous boss?

   David (Sonny) Werblin.

3. Joe correctly predicted the Jets' victory over the Colts in Super Bowl III. How many TD passes did Joe throw in the game?

   None. The Jets got a TD run from Matt Snell and three Jim Turner field goals in a 16-7 victory.

4. Joe's biggest passing game was a 496-yard effort against Baltimore in 1972. Only two NFL quarterbacks have ever thrown for more than 500 yards in a game. Name them.

   Norm Van Brocklin (554 yards for the Rams vs. the New York Yanks in 1951) and Y. A. Tittle (505 yards for the Giants vs. the Redskins in 1962).

5. No one has ever come close to Joe's record of 4,007 yards passing in a season. When did Namath set the record?

   1967. Unfortunately the Jets finished 7-7 and missed the playoffs.

Bart Starr

1. How many Super Bowls did Bart play in?
   Two.

2. What role did Lisle Blackbourn and Scooter McLean play in Bart's career at Green Bay?
   They were his first two coaches—Blackbourn in 1956–57 and McLean in 1958—before Vince Lombardi arrived in Wisconsin.

3. How many times did Starr lead the NFL in passing?
   Three times—1962, '64, and '66.

4. Who did Bart succeed as Green Bay coach?
   Dan Devine.

5. What Bart's real first name?
   Bryan.

John Unitas

1. Where did John finish his playing career?
   The all-time Baltimore great ended his playing days with the San Diego Chargers.

2. Though John starred for the Colts from 1956 to 1972, he failed in his first NFL trial in 1955. Which team cut the great Unitas?
   The Pittsburgh Steelers.

3. Johnny U. is the NFL's all-time passing yardage leader. How many yards did he throw for: More than 30,000? More than 35,000? More than 40,000?

More than 40,000 — 40,239 to be exact. Fran Tarkenton is in second place.

4. When Johnny led the Colts to the 1958 title — in the famous overtime game — it made a champion of his roly-poly coach. Name the coach, who later won a Super Bowl with the Jets.

Wilbur "Weeb" Ewbank.

5. One Unitas record is likely to last forever. He threw a TD pass in every game for nearly four seasons. How many games did that cover?

47 straight. Second-place is held by Daryle Lamonica with only 25!

Gale Sayers

1. An All-American at the University of Kansas, Gale starred for which pro team?

Chicago Bears.

2. Though a series of knee injuries cut his career short, Gale still managed to become the all-time No. 2 man in yardage per carry. What was Sayers' average gain?

5 yards per carry (4,956 yards on 991 carries).

3. Name Sayers' teammate whose tragic story was told in the TV-movie *Brian's Song*.

Brian Piccolo.

4. Bears' opponents almost hated to score. That meant they'd have to kick off to Chicago — and Sayers! How many kickoffs did Gale return for TDs?

A record-tying six. He also had the highest lifetime average return with 30.56 yards on 91 attempts.

5. How many NFL championship games did Sayers play in?

None. In fact, the Bears had only two winning seasons in Gale's seven years with them.

The Name Game

Match the modern-day NFL star with his nickname:

1. Lance Alworth	a. Buck
2. Joe Namath	b. Jazz
3. Christian A. Jurgensen	c. Butch Cassidy
4. Junious Buchanan	d. Bambi
5. Joe Greene	e. Speedy
6. Marlin Briscoe	f. Broadway Joe
7. Larry Csonka	g. Jefferson St. Joe
8. Jim Kiick	h. Sonny
9. Roger Staubach	i. Mean Joe
10. Ed Jones	j. Juice
11. Orenthal J. Simpson	k. The Magician
12. Clarence Jackson	l. Sundance Kid
13. Leslie Duncan	m. Too Tall
14. Joe Gilliam	n. The Dodger
15. Ivan Frederickson	o. Deacon
16. Paul Hornung	p. Mercury
17. Charles Clark	q. Bam
18. David Jones	r. Golden Boy
19. Sam Cunningham	s. Tucker
20. Eugene Morris	t. Boobie

1:d; 2:f; 3:h; 4:a; 5:i; 6:k; 7:l; 8:c; 9:n; 10:m; 11:j; 12:b; 13:e; 14:g; 15:s; 16:r; 17:t; 18:o; 19:q; 20:p.

Weren't You. . . ?

Match these older pro stars with their famous nicknames:

1. Charlie Justice
2. Howard Cassady
3. Clyde Turner
4. Fred Williamson
5. Harold Grange
6. Earl H. Clark
7. Dick Lane
8. Fred Thruston
9. Alex Webster
10. DeWitt Coulter
11. Emlen Tunnell
12. Dan Towler
13. John McNally
14. George Halas
15. Paul Younger
16. R. C. Owens
17. Bob Hoernschemeyer
18. Frank Davidson
19. Elroy Hirsch
20. Earl Girard

a. Alley-Oop
b. The Gremlin
c. Deacon
d. Choo Choo
e. Crazy Legs
f. Jug
g. Hopalong
h. Hunchy
i. Cotton
j. Bulldog
k. Tank
l. The Hammer
m. Red
n. Night Train
o. Big Red
p. Poppa Bear
q. Johnny Blood
r. Tex
s. Fuzzy
t. Dutch

1:d; 2:g; 3:j; 4:l; 5:m; 6:t; 7:n; 8:s; 9:o; 10:r; 11:b; 12:c; 13:q; 14:p; 15:k; 16:a; 17:h; 18:i; 19:e; 20:f.

Who Am I?

Identify these future Hall-of-Famers from the descriptions:

1. I was Chicago's tough middle linebacker for nine years before a crippling knee injury ended my career.

2. My great speed and quickness enabled me to overcome my lack of size (6-0, 182). My teammates at San Diego and Dallas called me Bambi. I caught 542 passes for 10,267 yards, an 18.9 average.

3. We were the "Mr. Inside" and "Mr. Outside" of the champion Packers. The little one was called "The Golden Boy"; the big one was simply Jim.

4. I don't plan on the Hall of Fame for a long time — not as long as I can lead the Steelers' defense. They call me "Mean" but I'm really a pussycat!

5. I've scrambled my way around the NFL's big guys for years — and haven't missed a game through injury. Though I spent a few years with the Giants, I'm best known as the Vikings' quarterback in a couple of Super Bowls.

6. Rams' opponents rarely ran to my side of the defensive line. Though I spent the last years of my career with San Diego and Washington, I was still known as the "Deacon" of defensive ends.

7. In 1964 the Eagles traded me to Washington for Norm Snead. They goofed. I led the 'Skins for many years thereafter. They tell me there's no one better at scoring in the closing minutes. My real name is Christian Adolph, but I'm better known by my nickname.

8. I made middle linebacker a popular position. I starred in a TV special about my "Violent World" and led the Giants' defense for nearly 10 seasons before a trade to Washington.

9. You'll find me right in the middle of Minnesota's Purple People Eaters. My buddies Eller and Marshall have helped me stop opposing runners for years.

10. I played in three Super Bowls with Green Bay and Dallas. But I'm best remembered for my play as the Packers' cornerback under Vince Lombardi. I intercepted 48 passes during my 12 NFL seasons.

11. At 6-0 and 190, they said I was too small for the NFL grind. I showed 'em. I practically invented the safety blitz and killed Cardinal opponents for 13 years. Along the way I intercepted 52 passes.

12. I've been playing defensive tackle for the Rams since 1962. I love it—especially since my brother Phil began playing alongside. Very few opponents pass my 6-5, 272-pound body.

13. When the Browns cut me after the 1961 season, some experts said I was through. But I found a home with the Chiefs and

became one of the AFL's top quarterbacks for more than a decade. I helped KC in two Super Bowl appearances.

14. I was an AFL original after graduating from Southern Cal. As a 6-4, 249-pound offensive tackle I constantly opened holes in the opponents' line. My team? The Chargers for 10 seasons and the Raiders for one. Now I'm a lawyer and I ran a WFL club in 1974.

15. Upon arriving at Kansas City in 1967 I took over at middle linebacker and stayed there from then on. Most experts agree that I've been the best middle linebacker in football since then.

16. Too old? That's what they said when I was cut by the Bears in 1958. But I joined the Oilers as a quarterback and kicker in 1960 and I've been doing my thing ever since, with Houston and Oakland. I'm the only pro to have played in four decades—the 40's, 50's, 60's, and 70's.

17. I became the Packers' defensive end in 1960, just in time to take part in their fabulous decade under Vince Lombardi. People often confused me with our great safety, Willie Wood. But both of us Willies were great.

1. Dick Butkus; 2. Lance Alworth; 3. Paul Hornung and Jim Taylor; 4. "Mean" Joe Greene; 5. Fran Tarkenton; 6. David "Deacon" Jones; 7. "Sonny" Jurgensen; 8. Sam Huff; 9. Alan Page; 10. Herb Adderley; 11. Larry Wilson; 12. Merlin Olsen; 13. Len Dawson; 14. Ron Mix; 15. Willie Lanier; 16. George Blanda; 17. Willie Davis.

"Immortal" Questions

Mel Hein

1. Before coming to the New York Giants, Mel starred at which West Coast school?
Washington State.

2. The Giants had great success with Mel at center and linebacker. How many division titles did they win?
Seven.

3. How many touchdowns did Mel score as a pro?
One. He returned an interception 50 yards against Green Bay in 1938.

4. How many championship squads did he play on?
Two.

5. The Giants retired Mel's number at the end of his career. What was it?
Seven.

Otto Graham

1. Otto starred in both the All-American Conference and the NFL. In 10 pro seasons, how many times did he lead the league in passing?
Six.

2. Where did Graham play college football?
Northwestern. He also starred in basketball there.

3. How many NFL Pro Bowls did Otto play in ?

   Five, from the 1950 through 1954 seasons.

4. Which pro team did Otto coach?

   The Washington Redskins.

5. Both before and after his pro coaching stint, Otto coached at the college level. Where?

   The Coast Guard Academy.

Red Grange

1. Red had several nicknames, including "The Wheaton Iceman" and "The Galloping Ghost." What was his given name?

   Harold.

2. Red made history at the University of Illinois by scoring four touchdowns in 12 minutes. Who were the opponents?

   The Wolverines of Michigan. In the same 12 minutes, Grange accounted for 303 yards.

3. When did Red break into the pros?

   On Thanksgiving Day, 1925. He and the Chicago Bears attracted 36,000 fans, the largest pro crowd ever to that date.

4. Who was the notorious showman-promoter who directed Grange's career?

   C. C. (Cash-and-Carry) Pyle.

5. When did Red's pro career end?

   1935.

Ernie Nevers

1. As a player at Stanford, Ernie played in the Rose Bowl against which midwestern power?

   Notre Dame, led by the famed Four Horsemen.

2. Ernie also played major league baseball. As a pitcher for the St. Louis Browns, he played a part in one of baseball's greatest records. Which one?

   He gave up home runs number 8 and 41 in Babe Ruth's 60-homer season (1927).

3. Which NFL team did Nevers first play for?

   The Duluth (Minn.) Eskimos, often called Ernie Nevers' Eskimos.

4. His greatest day in pro football was Thanksgiving Day, 1929. What did he do?

   Ernie's Chicago Cardinals wiped out their arch-rivals, the Bears, 40-6. Ernie's part? He scored all 40 points, an all-time record!

5. How did Ernie get his nickname, "The Iron Man"?

   His Eskimos once played 29 games from September to January, including five in eight days. Nevers missed only 27 of the 1,740 minutes in those games.

Bronko Nagurski

1. What was Bronko's real name?

   Here's a mild surprise. It was—Bronko!

2. Where did he play college football?

   The University of Minnesota.

3. When Bronko graduated, the New York Giants offered him $7,500 a season to play with them. But he'd already signed a pro contract. With whom?

   The Chicago Bears.

4. A wobbly fourth-down Nagurski-to-Red Grange pass gave the Bears the 1932 pro championship. Where was the game played?

   Indoors in Chicago Stadium. The field was only 80 yards long.

5. In 1937, the Bronk retired from pro football though he still had many good years left. Why?

   He was making too much money wrestling. He came back to football during World War II when many players were drafted into the service.

The Numbers Game

Baseball has its famous uniform numbers. No. 3 on the Yankees? Sure, Babe Ruth. Football numbers become famous, too. Try to identify each player from his team and uniform number.

1. No. 39, Miami Dolphins _____

2. No. 12, New York Jets _____

3. No. 32, Buffalo Bills _____

4. No. 10, Minnesota Vikings _____

5. No. 12, Oakland Raiders _____

6. No. 5, Philadelphia
   Eagles _____

7. No. 75, Pittsburgh Steelers _____

8. No. 43, Washington
   Redskins _____

9. No. 22, Dallas Cowboys _____

10. No. 1, Miami Dolphins _____

11. No. 44, Denver Broncos _____

12. No. 00, Oakland Raiders _____

Answers: 1. Larry Csonka; 2. Joe Namath; 3. O. J. Simpson; 4. Fran Tarkenton; 5. Ken Stabler; 6. Roman Gabriel; 7. Mean Joe Greene; 8. Larry Brown; 9. Bob Hayes; 10. Garo Yepremian; 11. Floyd Little; 12. Jim Otto.

Supers of the Past

Here's a toughie. Match the pro Hall-of-Famer with his college, then add his pro team. (Hint: Four were Bears, three Eagles, two Redskins, Colts, Giants, Rams, and Packers, and one Lion, Brown, and Cardinal).

1. Sammy Baugh	a.	Notre Dame
2. Gino Marchetti	b.	Alabama
3. Ken Strong	c.	Indiana
4. Wayne Millner	d.	Washington St.
5. Sid Luckman	e.	NYU
6. Jim Parker	f.	Duke
7. Bob Waterfield	g.	Syracuse
8. Tony Canadeo	h.	Georgia
9. Elroy Hirsch	i.	TCU
10. Jack Christiansen	j.	Colgate
11. Bulldog Turner	k.	LSU
12. Jim Brown	l.	San Francisco
13. Pete Pihos	m.	UCLA
14. Don Hutson	n.	Penn
15. Steve Van Buren	o.	Colorado St.
16. Mel Hein	p.	Columbia
17. George McAfee	q.	Gonzaga
18. Chuck Bednarik	r.	Hardin-Simmons
19. Danny Fortmann	s.	Wisconsin
20. Charlie Trippi	t.	Ohio State

aa. Cardinals	ff.	Lions
bb. Browns	gg.	Rams
cc. Packers	hh.	Bears
dd. Eagles	ii.	Redskins
ee. Giants	jj.	Colts

1-i-ii, 2-l-jj, 3-e-ee, 4-a-ii, 5-p-hh, 6-t-jj, 7-m-gg, 8-q-cc, 9-s-gg, 10-o-ff, 11-r-hh, 12-g-bb, 13-c-dd, 14-b-cc, 15-k-dd, 16-d-ee, 17-f-hh, 18-n-dd, 19-j-hh, 10-h-aa.

Hooray For Hollywood

When you visit your local theater, you may get to see your favorite NFL star. Many of them are headed for the movies — and TV, too. Identify the following stars from the descriptions:

1. Name the former defensive back who went on to star on TV's *Julia*, as Spearchucker in the movie *M*A*S*H*, and as the star of *Three the Hard Way*.

2. What former defensive tackle played the role of Mongo in *Blazing Saddles*?

3. What former quarterback — and Monday night football analyst — has starred in several episodes of *Police Story*?

4. Who's the Buffalo running back who had a major role in *The Towering Inferno*?

5. The NFL's all-time leading rusher has starred in numerous movies, including *Ice Station Zebra*, *The Dirty Dozen*, and *Tick, Tick, Tick*. Name this great Cleveland Brown star.

1. Fred "The Hammer" Williamson; 2. Alex Karras; 3. Don Meredith; 4. O. J. Simpson; 5. Jim Brown.

WHISTLES AND FLAGS

Men in the Striped Shirts

1. What do the following men have in common: Tommy Bell, Pat Haggerty, Norm Schachter, Ben Dreith, and Bernie Ulman?

   All are referees in the National Football League.

2. It takes six officials to run an NFL game. What are their formal titles?

   Referee, umpire, head linesman, line judge, back judge, and field judge.

3. Which official stands right behind the defensive line?

   The umpire.

4. Which official marks the ball ready for play and stands behind the offensive team?

   The referee.

5. Which official holds the front stake in measuring for first downs?

   The head linesman. The actual call is made by the referee.

6. The official time for NFL games is kept on the scoreboard clock. Should that clock fail to work, the time is kept on the field by one of the officials. Which one?

   The line judge.

7. Who is the NFL's Supervisor of Officials?

   Art McNally.

8. Can you name the charter member of pro football's Hall of Fame who later became an American (baseball) League umpire?

Cal Hubbard, who played with the Giants, Packers, and Steelers from 1927 to 1936.

9. A quarterback with the Colts and Eagles from 1950 to 1956 is now one of the top back judges in the NFL. Name him.

Adrian Burk.

10. Until 1965, NFL games were officiated by five men. Which official became the sixth member of the officiating team?

The line judge.

Waiting for the Signals

Did you ever try to guess, in advance, what penalty will be called? That's the best you *can* do—guess! Nothing happens until the referee gives the official signal. Look at each signal and identify the call:

1. Offside (or encroachment); 2. Personal foul; 3. Safety; 4. Holding; 5. Time out; 6. Clipping; 7. Interference; 8. Ineligible receiver downfield.

What's the Call, Ref?

In April, 1974, the NFL owners voted several exciting new changes in the playing rules. Answer these questions based on those changes:

1. Sudden death, which had been used only in playoff games, was added for pre- and regular-season contests. The owners, however, limited the rule. How?

    Only one 15-minute overtime is played. If the score is still tied, it goes into the books as a tie. Championship games, of course, are still played to a decision.

2. The goal posts were returned to the end line for the first time since 1933. How far beyond the goal line is the end line?

    Ten yards.

3. The penalty for offensive holding was reduced from 15 yards. What's the penalty now?

    Ten yards.

4. The punt coverage rules also came in for change. How many members of the punting team are now allowed to move downfield before the ball is kicked?

    Two.

5. The new punt-coverage rule brought back an almost forgotten style of punting. What was it?

    The coffin-corner kick. The punter tries to kick the ball out of bounds as close to the goal line as possible.

6. The same two-man coverage rule also applies to what other type of kick?

Field goals.

7. Under the new rules, how many times may a defensive back hit ("chuck") a receiver on his way downfield?

Once.

8. Kickoffs are now made from the kicking team's 35-yard line. Where was the ball kicked from before?

The 40-yard line.

9. On most missed field goals, the ball is now returned to the line of scrimmage. What are the exceptions?

On kicks from inside the 20-yard line, the ball is returned to the 20.

10. In an important change, wide receivers are no longer permitted to block back below the waist. What dangerous type of block did this new rule eliminate?

Crack-back block.

ALL OVER THE FIELD

What's the Good Word?

Football, like all sports, has a language all its own. Figure out these football terms from the descriptions:

1. What do you call a defensive lineman who plays directly in front of the offensive center?

   A nose guard or middle guard.

2. What do you call a running back who sets up at the back of the I formation?

   Tailback.

3. What do you call a back who sets up between the tackle and wide receiver?

   Slotback.

4. What is it called when one or more linebackers rush the passer?

   Blitz or red dog.

5. What do you call the defensive back who has no specific assignment but roams around for an interception?

   Free safety.

6. What do you call the defensive alignment where a linebacker sets up right behind a lineman?

   Stack.

7. What one word is used to describe the cornerbacks and safeties?

   Secondary.

8. What do you call a kickoff which bounces along the ground?

   Squib.

9. What term is applied to the players who work on kickoffs, punts, and extra points?

   Special teams, bomb squad, or suicide squad.

10. The punt receiver waves his right hand high above his head. What is he doing?

    Signaling for a fair catch.

11. In an attempt to recover the ball, the kickoff team boots the ball just more than 10 yards. What are they doing?

    Making an onside kick.

12. The kickoff sails through the end zone. The officials place it at the 20-yard line. Why?

    It's a touchback.

13. What do you call a very long pass?

    A bomb.

14. There are two ways to set up for a forward pass. The quarterback can drop back. What's the other way?

    Roll out or sprint out.

15. What do you call the play in which the quarterback fakes a handoff, hides the ball behind his leg, and runs?

    Bootleg.

16. What do you call the spot where the play begins?

    Line of scrimmage.

17. The defensive back moves right up to the line of scrimmage, hits the receiver right away to knock him off-stride, then tries to stay with him. What is this technique called?

Bump-and-run.

18. The punter tries to kick out of bounds near the goal line. What is this technique called?

Going for the coffin corner.

19. When a team must score in the closing moments, it often uses a special technique designed to save time. What is it called?

The two-minute drill.

20. In the two-minute drill, the opponents often counter by dropping their backs and linebackers very deep. What is this defense called?

The prevent defense.

Hey, Boss!

Coaches and players come and go. But owners—they seem to be around forever! Here are some famous NFL head men. Identify their teams in the spaces provided.

1. Art Rooney   _____

2. George Halas   _____

3. Wellington Mara   _____

4. Carroll Rosenbloom   _____

5. Lamar Hunt   _____

6. Joe Robbie   _____

7. Bud Adams   _____

8. Art Modell   _____

9. Al Davis   _____

10. Clint Murchison   _____

1. Rooney—Pittsburgh Steelers; 2. Halas—Chicago Bears; 3. Mara—New York Giants; 4. Rosenbloom—L. A. Rams; 5. Hunt—Kansas City Chiefs; 6. Robbie—Miami Dolphins; 7. Adams—Houston Oilers; 8. Modell—Cleveland Browns; 9. Davis—Oakland Raiders; 10. Murchison—Dallas Cowboys.

All in the Family

Dozens of brother combinations have starred in football and other sports. Identify the following sets of brothers from the descriptions:

1. The Ram defensive tackles, one an all-time All-Pro. Both starred at Utah State. The younger brother is now a Denver Bronco.

2. The San Francisco defensive back whose brother Brian is a star guard with the New York Nets.

3. The Giant running back whose brother Alex won an American League batting championship.

4. The Raider guard whose brother Marvin is an excellent Kansas City defensive end.

5. The Jet wide receiver whose brother Melvin starred as QB for Mississippi State.

6. The Giant place-kicker whose brother Charley kicked for the Redskins and Patriots.

7. The Detroit Lion running star whose brother Miller was a great defensive back for Denver, Houston, and St. Louis. Their cousin, Jerry LeVias, is a San Diego wide receiver.

8. The Atlanta Falcon kicker whose brother Steve, also a place-kicker, was San Francisco's third-round draft choice in 1975.

9. The former Detroit Lion defensive tackle, now a top TV color analyst, whose brother Ted starred as an offensive lineman for Pittsburgh and Chicago.

10. The Dolphins' super defensive back whose brother Bobby was a versatile offensive back for the Broncos.

11. The Buffalo Bills' tight end and tackle whose brother Jim was a great wide receiver for Notre Dame and the Chicago Bears.

12. The Oakland defensive lineman whose brother Tody played defensive end for Southern Cal, the Cowboys, and the Oilers.

1. Merlin and Phil Olsen; 2. Bruce and Brian Taylor; 3. Ron and Alex Johnson; 4. Gene and Marvin Upshaw; 5. Jerome and Melvin Barkum; 6. Pete and Charley Gogolak; 7. Mel and Miller Farr; 8. Nick and Steve Mike-Mayer; 9. Alex and Ted Karras; 10. Dick and Bobby Anderson; 11. Paul and Jim Seymour; 12. Bubba and Tody Smith.

Brawn—and Brains

What positions did the following NFL coaches play during their pro careers?

1. Bart Starr?

   That's easy. Starr, the Packer coach, was the Packers' star quarterback for 16 years.

2. Jack Pardee?

   The Bears' coach was an all-pro linebacker for the Rams and Redskins over 15 super seasons.

3. Don Shula?

   The Dolphins' boss was a stellar defensive back with the Browns and Colts for seven years.

4. Lou Saban?

   A top-notch linebacker, Lou helped the Browns win four All-America Conference championships from 1946–49.

5. Tom Landry?

   The Dallas coach played some halfback and quarterback but mostly defensive back in six seasons with the Giants.

6. Dick Nolan?

   Throughout a nine-season NFL career, Dick was an outstanding defensive back for the Giants, Cards, and Cowboys.

7. Forrest Gregg?

   During 15 NFL years, offensive tackle Gregg played in three Super Bowls with the Packers and Cowboys.

8. Ted Marchibroda?

   The Colts' leader was a quarterback for the Steelers and Cards during four NFL years.

9. Chuck Noll?

   The coach who led Pittsburgh to the Super Bowl played linebacker and guard for Paul Brown's Cleveland Browns.

10. Mike McCormack?

    A teammate of Noll's, McCormack starred at offensive tackle for 10 years, nine with the Browns.

Thou Shalt Pass

You're the play-by-play analyst. Describe the following routes run by a receiver:

1. He runs straight downfield, then cuts to the sideline.

   Down-and-out.

2. He runs directly toward the marker located where the goal line and sideline meet.

   Flag pattern.

3. He goes all out and sprints right past the defenders.

   Fly pattern.

4. He runs about 10 yards downfield, fakes the opponent deep, and comes back for the pass.

   Hook pattern.

5. He runs straight downfield, then curves back toward the line of scrimmage.

   Curl pattern.

6. He runs at an angle toward the opposite side of the field, passing a teammate along the way.

   Crossing pattern.

Around the League

1. Which pro team last completed an entire season undefeated?

   The 1972 Miami Dolphins. They went on to defeat Washington in the Super Bowl, completing a perfect 17-0 year.

2. How wide is the football field?

   160 feet, or $53\frac{1}{3}$ yards.

3. How far apart are the hashmarks?

   18 feet, six inches, the same width as the goal posts.

4. What NFL team wears uniforms of seal brown, orange, and white?

   The Cleveland Browns.

5. What team wears scarlet, Columbia blue, and white?

   The Houston Oilers.

6. Aqua and orange?

   The Miami Dolphins.

7. Honolulu blue and silver?

   The Detroit Lions.

8. George Blanda played the most seasons in the NFL. But who coached the most seasons?

   Another George—George Halas. Old Poppa Bear led the team he owned, the Bears, for 40 years (1920-29, 1933-42, 1946-55, and 1958-67).

9. Who led his league in scoring the most years?

Don Hutson, Green Bay's immortal receiver, topped the NFL for five straight years, 1940-44. Boston Patriot kicker-receiver Gino Cappelletti matched Hutson's total, leading the AFL in 1961, '63, '64, '65, and '66.

10. Who scored the most points in one season?

Green Bay's Golden Boy, Paul Hornung. He racked up 176 points in 1960 on 15 touchdowns, 41 points-after, and 15 field goals.

11. Only one player has ever scored 40 points in a game. Name him.

Hall-of-Famer Ernie Nevers of the Chicago Cardinals tallied six TDs and four extra points against the crosstown rival Bears on Nov. 28, 1929. The six six-pointers set a single game record, since tied by Cleveland's Dub Jones (1951) and the Bears' Gale Sayers (1965).

12. Lou Groza was one of the finest kickers in NFL history. What was his appropriate nickname?

"The Toe."

13. Groza was no kicking freak. He was a key man in the Cleveland Browns' offense. What position did he play?

Tackle.

14. Which of the following place-kickers utilize soccer style: David Ray, Chester Marcol, George Blanda, Tom Dempsey, Garo Yepremian, Jan Stenerud, Fred Cox.

The sidewheelers are Marcol, Yepremian, and Stenerud.

15. Who kicked the longest field goal in pro history?

Tom Dempsey, then of the New Orleans Saints, booted a 63-yarder on Nov. 8, 1970. The last-second, sub-orbital kick beat the Detroit Lions.

16. Only one defensive player has ever scored two safeties in one game. Name him.

Los Angeles end Fred Dryer scored two two-pointers against Green Bay, Oct. 21, 1973. Amazingly, only six players have scored as many as two safeties in a *season!*

17. Who ran for the most touchdowns in one season?

The champion Packers' Jim Taylor rushed for 19 scores in 1962.

18. Sonny Jurgensen had his busiest year in 1967, throwing a record 508 passes. What's Sonny's real name?

Christian Adolph Jurgensen.

19. Of the 508 passes, how many did Jurgy complete?

288, another NFL single-season record.

20. Who was the most accurate passer in history?

Bart Starr of Green Bay. In over 16 NFL seasons, Bart completed 1,808 of 3,149 passes, a 57.4% mark.

21. Which quarterback threw the most passes in one game?

The Grand Old Man, George Blanda, tossed 68 aerials for Houston against Buffalo in 1964. He completed 37.

22. Only one QB has ever thrown for more than 4,000 yards in one season. Name him.

   Joe Namath and his Jet receivers accounted for 4,007 yards in 1967. For mileage freaks, that's more than $2\frac{1}{4}$ miles.

23. Who was the most intercepted passer in NFL history?

   It's Old George Blanda, again. He was picked off a record 42 times in one season (1962) and 276 times in his lengthy career with Chicago, Baltimore, Houston, and Oakland.

24. Which receiver led the NFL the most seasons?

   Don Hutson of Green Bay. He topped league pass catchers eight times (1936, '37, '39, and 1941 through '45). The five-year streak also set an all-time record.

25. Who caught the most passes in history?

   Don Maynard, who spent most of his career with the Jets, caught 633, two more than Baltimore superstar Raymond Berry.

26. How many yards did Maynard account for?

   A record 11,834 yards, almost 2,000 more than runner-up Lance Alworth.

27. Who caught the most touchdown passes?

   That man Don Hutson again. He grabbed 99 six-point passes in 11 seasons at Green Bay.

28. Sammy Baugh was one of the greatest passers of all time. But he also shares a super defensive record. What is it?

Most interceptions in one game, four.
Thirteen others, including Dolphin Dick
Anderson, share the mark.

29. Who was the NFL's all-time best inter-
ceptor?

Emlen Tunnell, the Giants' Hall-of-
Famer. In 11 years with New York and
three with Green Bay, Tunnell grabbed
off 79 errant passes, returning them for a
record 1,282 yards.

30. Defensive back Charley McNeil was San
Diego's most offensive player on Sept.
24, 1961. How did he do it?

He returned misfired Houston passes for
a record 177 yards. That performance
helped McNeil set a single-season record
of 349 yards on intercepted passes.

31. The record for the longest punt may
never be broken. Who holds it and what
is it?

Steve O'Neal of the New York Jets
boomed a 98-yarder on Sept. 21, 1969.
Following the snap from the Jet 1-yard
line, O'Neal boomed the punt from deep
in his end zone to the Denver Broncos' 1.

32. Bob Scarpitto was the busiest man in
Denver in 1967. Why?

Punter Scarpitto was forced to bail the
last-place Broncos out of trouble a record
105 times!

33. Scarpitto's punting enabled Rodger Bird
of Oakland to establish an NFL record for
punt returns in one game. What is it?

Bird returned a record nine punts in the Sept. 10, 1967, Oakland-Denver game. San Francisco's Ralph McGill tied the mark on Oct. 29, 1967.

34. Who holds the record for most fair catches in a game?

Miami's Jake Scott. The Dolphin star took six against Buffalo on Dec. 20, 1970.

35. Who had the most punt-return yardage in one game?

Oakland's George Atkinson, who gained 205 yards on Buffalo punts on Sept. 15, 1968.

36. Only two players have returned two punts for touchdowns in a single game. Name them.

Dick Christy of the old New York Titans in 1962 and Jack Christiansen. Detroit's Christiansen did it twice in one season — against the Rams on Oct. 14, 1951, and against the Packers on Nov. 22, 1951. The current Stanford coach also holds the all-time records for TD returns in a season (4) and a career (8).

37. Oakland trounced Kansas City, 44-22, on Nov. 23, 1967. Along the way, the Raiders enabled KC's Noland Smith to set an all-time record. What was it?

Smith returned nine Oakland kickoffs.

38. Ollie Matson, Gale Sayers, and Travis Williams share an NFL record. What is it?

The Cards' Matson, the Bears' Sayers, and the Packers' and Rams' Williams each returned six kickoffs for touchdowns. Williams' four in one season set a record, since tied by Chicago's Cecil Turner.

39. "Old Butterfingers"? Believe it or not, that would be a fine nickname for John Unitas. How many times did Unitas fumble during his career?

An all-time record 95. He also recovered 29 fumbles, tied for second in that category.

40. Who is number-one in fumbles recovered?

Jack Kemp of the Steelers, Chargers, and Bills. The old quarterback, now a U.S. Congressman, picked up 38 during his 10-year career.

41. Who holds the record for the longest fumble return?

Oakland Raider Jack Tatum. He ran 104 yards with a Green Bay bobble on Sept. 24, 1972.

42. Tatum's run broke one of the NFL's oldest records, a 98-yard return on Nov. 4, 1923. Who owned the old mark?

Chicago owner-coach-player George Halas.

43. Corwin Clatt, Vic Sears, and Ed Beatty share an NFL record. What is it?

Each recovered three fumbles in one game.

44. The Redskins downed the Giants 72-41 on Nov. 27, 1966, the highest scoring NFL game ever. In addition, Washington set the regular-season one-team record of

72 points with a field goal on the last play. Name the 'Skin coach who called for the extra score. (Hint: He was Cleveland's all-time great quarterback.)

Otto Graham.

45. Though Pittsburgh racked up two touchdowns to the Cardinals' one on Sept. 24, 1967, the Cards still won by 14 points. How?

St. Louis kicked a record seven field goals (on a record nine attempts) for 21 points and a 28-14 victory.

46. The 1966 Rams raced to 38 first downs on their way to a 55-14 win on Nov. 13, 1966. The losers must've been uncomfortable, 3,000 miles away from their Yankee Stadium home. Name the losing team.

New York Giants.

Two for the Money

It takes a great athlete to play in the National Football League. It takes even more ability to excel in two sports. Identify these two-sport stars who played in the NFL:

1. The Packers' safety during the Lombardi era who also played first base for the Washington Senators.

2. The Dallas and Green Bay punter who was a college basketball All-America and played in the A. B. A.

3. The two-year Denver defensive back (1966–67) who went on to stardom in the A. B. A.

4. The great Cowboy and 49er wide receiver who won two gold medals in the 1964 Tokyo Olympic games.

5. Best known as the only man to pinch-hit for Ted Williams, he played one year for the 49ers and is now the Broncos' Director of Scouting.

6. The Dallas running back who stars as a rodeo cowboy in the off-season.

7. An outstanding college and pro footballer, he also starred in basketball at the U. of Colorado. His best game? Making big decisions—as a Justice of the U. S. Supreme Court!

8. An outstanding defensive lineman with the Chiefs and Oilers, he won an NCAA wrestling championship at Arizona State.

1. Tom Brown; 2. Ron Widby; 3. Lonnie Wright; 4. Bob Hayes; 5. Carroll Hardy; 6. Walt Garrison; 7. Byron "Whizzer" White; 8. Curley Culp.

Weird Moments

1. The 1934 NFL championship game was played on a frozen field at New York's Polo Grounds. The Bears took an early lead. But the Giants did something late in the game that enabled them to pull out the victory. What did they do?

   They changed their footwear from cleats to sneakers. This prevented them from slipping and sliding on the frozen turf. They went on to win, 30-13.

2. In 1964, a Minnesota Viking defensive end picked up a fumble and ran the wrong way. He downed the ball in his own end zone, thus scoring a safety for the rival 49ers. Name the erring player, a future all-pro.

   Jim Marshall. His goof didn't hurt the Vikes. They still won, 27-22.

3. The rookie coach was in his first game in the NFL. His Packers were up against the Giants. A New York running play swept right into the sideline where the coach was flattened, breaking his leg. Name this unfortunate coach, now the head man at Notre Dame.

   Dan Devine. To make matters worse, the Giants won the game 42-40.

THE BIG GAMES

The First 34 Years

Until the AFL and the Super Bowl came along, the NFL championship game determined the best team in pro football. Answer these questions about those 34 great games:

1. Which team played in the most NFL championship games?

   The New York Giants. They took part in the first three (1933-35) and eleven more through 1963, a record total of 14.

2. Which team appeared in the most consecutive games?

   The Cleveland Browns. In its first six years in the NFL (1950–55) Cleveland played in all *six* championship games.

3. Which team won the most games?

   Green Bay and Chicago won six each. The Packers then won two additional NFL championships in 1966 and 1967 (after the Super Bowl began).

4. Which team lost the most championships?

   It's not even close. The Giants lost 11 of their 14 title game appearances.

5. What was the highest total points scored by a team in one game?

   73 by the 1940 Chicago Bears. Their 73-0 rout of the Redskins stands as one of the most memorable games in NFL history.

6. Two teams combined to score 73 points in a title game, tying the 1940 Chicago-Washington record. Which two teams?

Detroit and Cleveland. The Lions routed the Browns 59-14 in the 1957 game.

7. The fewest points scored in an NFL championship — seven — occurred during the 1948 Blizzard Bowl game. Which teams played?

Philadelphia scored the lone TD to defeat the Chicago Cardinals, 7-0. The following year, Philadelphia topped Los Angeles, 14-0, the second fewest number of points scored.

8. Who was the leading pass receiver in all title games?

Dante Lavelli of the Browns. He grabbed 24 aerials in six games.

9. Which passer and receiver combined for the longest pass play in history?

Ram quarterback Bob Waterfield threw an 82-yard bomb to Glenn Davis in the 1950 game against Cleveland.

10. Speaking of receivers, who caught the most TD passes in one game?

Cleveland's Gary Collins grabbed three six-pointers in the 1964 game against Baltimore. Three Lou Groza conversions and two Groza field goals gave the Browns a solid 27-0 win.

11. Groza, known as "The Toe," kicked the longest field goal in title game history. How long was it?

52 yards, in 1951. Unfortunately his Browns still lost to Los Angeles, 24-17.

12. Who rushed for the most yards in one game?

Steve Van Buren. His 196 yards on 31 carries helped the Eagles defeat the Rams, 14-0, in 1949.

13. The title game record for longest run from scrimmage was set *twice* in the 1947 championship. Who set it?

Elmer Angsman of the Chicago Cardinals. He ran 70 yards for a touchdown, then came right back and duplicated the feat. His two TDs helped Chicago defeat Philadelphia, 28-21.

14. In the same game, the Eagles' quarterback set the record for most passes and completions. Who was he?

Tommy Thompson. He hit on 27 of 44 tries.

15. Some experts call the 1958 championship tilt "The Greatest Game Ever Played." Which two teams played?

The Colts and Giants. Baltimore tied New York in the closing seconds of the fourth quarter, then won in overtime.

16. Who scored the Colts' winning TD?

Fullback Alan Ameche.

17. Quarterback Johnny Unitas set a record for most passing yardage in that game. How many yards did John pass for?

349 on 26 completions in 40 attempts.

18. Here one for real trivia experts: Who was the Colts' kicker who tied the game?

Steve Myhra.

19. Sid Luckman, the Bears' great passer, holds the record for TD passes in one championship game with five. But he didn't set it in the 1940 73-0 win over the Redskins. When did he establish the mark?

1943. Luckman's five scoring tosses helped the Bears win 41-21 over—who else?—the Redskins!

20. Who won the first NFL championship game?

The Chicago Bears. They edged the Giants, 23-21, before 26,000 fans at Chicago on Dec. 17, 1933. The winning shares? Each Bear player received $210.34.

21. A Giant star set the still-standing record for most punts in that first game. Name this all-around performer.

Ken Strong.

22. How many kickoffs have been returned for touchdowns in NFL championship games?

None. The longest return was a 70-yarder by Max Krause of the Redskins against the Bears in 1940.

23. In the pre-Super Bowl days, only one punt was returned for a TD in NFL title play. Who did it?

Charlie Trippi of the Chicago Cardinals. His 75-yarder helped the Cards defeat the Eagles, 28-21, in 1947.

24. An all-pro passer holds the record for longest punting average in a game. Name him.

Sammy Baugh. The Redskins' quarterback for nearly two decades, Baugh punted six times for 52.5 yards in 1942 against Chicago.

25. Which quarterback threw the most passes in one game without an interception?

The Packers' star, Bart Starr. He tried 34 passes against Philadelphia in 1960 without being intercepted. Still, the Ealges, led by Norm Van Brocklin, won 17-13.

Behind the Mike

There's hardly a radio or TV booth in America that doesn't feature an ex-player describing the action. Identify the following well-known player-broadcasters:

1. The former San Francisco quarterback who describes AFC action.

   John Brodie.

2. The old New York Giant back who does the Monday night play-by-play.

   Frank Gifford.

3. The former Giant and Cardinal kicker who is CBS's top man on NFC coverage.

   Pat Summerall.

4. The one-time Giant lineman who often predicts plays on his AFC telecasts.

   Al DeRogatis.

5. The dandy Dallas quarterback who switched from ABC to NBC.

   Don Meredith.

6. The former Jet offensive lineman, often seen with Charlie Jones on AFC games.

   Sam DeLuca.

7. The excellent Eagle defensive back who does NFC games with Summerall.

   Tom Brookshier.

8. The immortal Baltimore quarterback who went right from the San Diego Chargers to CBS.

   Johnny Unitas.

9. The overly-large Detroit defensive tackle who replaced Meredith on Monday nights.

   Alex Karras.

10. The recently retired Redskin quarterback who now stars for CBS on Sundays.

    Sonny Jurgensen.

The Super Bowl

Super Bowl I, Los Angeles
January 15, 1967

1. Vince Lombardi's Green Bay Packers won Super Bowl I. Who lost?

   The Kansas City Chiefs, coached by Hank Stram.

2. Who scored the first Super Bowl touchdown ever?

   Packer receiver Max McGee. He took a short pass from Bart Starr and raced the rest of the 37 yards for the score.

3. Two Packers scored two touchdowns each in Super Bowl I. Who were they?

   Receiver McGee added a 13-yard TD reception to his 37-yard ice-breaker. Running back Elijah Pitts scored on five- and one-yard runs.

4. What was the final score?

   Packers 35, Chiefs 10.

5. An injury prevented an all-time Green Bay superstar from playing in Super Bowl I. In fact, he never played another game. Who was he?

   Immortal running back Paul Hornung.

Super Bowl II, Miami
January 14, 1968

1. Green Bay also won Super Bowl II. Which team lost?

   The Oakland Raiders.

2. Who coached Oakland?

John Rauch.

3. Green Bay took a 6-0 lead on two early field goals by their former punter. Name him.

Don Chandler. He kicked four field goals and three extra points — 15 points in all.

4. A Packer cornerback returned an intercepted pass 60 yards for a touchdown in Super Bowl II. He was the first defensive player to score in a Super Bowl. Name him.

Herb Adderley.

5. After the Super Bowl, Vince Lombardi quit as Packer coach. Who succeeded him?

Phil Bengtson.

Super Bowl III, Miami
January 12, 1969

1. Super Bowl III was the first that didn't involve the Green Bay Packers. Which two teams played?

The Baltimore Colts and the New York Jets. New York's 16-7 victory was the AFL's first.

2. Jet quarterback Joe Namath had a busy Super Bowl week. He guaranteed victory for his three-TD underdog team. And he nearly came to blows with Baltimore's kicker. Who was he?

Lou Michaels.

3. New York's Matt Snell scored on a four-yard run to give the Jets a 7-0 lead. It established an all-time first. What was it?

    It was the first time in Super Bowl history that the AFL had the lead.

4. Johnny Unitas wasn't the Baltimore starter. An injury kept him out of action most of the season. Who was his replacement? (Hint: He was the NFL's most valuable player.)

    Earl Morrall.

5. The Jets' win gave coach Weeb Ewbank a special place in history. Why?

    He became the first coach to win championships in both the NFL (with Baltimore in 1958 and 1959) and the AFL.

Super Bowl IV, New Orleans
January 11, 1970

1. Minnesota made its first Super Bowl appearance in Super Bowl IV. Who were the opponents?

    The Kansas City Chiefs, who also played in Super Bowl I.

2. Minnesota coach Bud Grant came to the club from Canada. So did the Vikings' quarterback. Who was he?

    Joe Kapp.

3. The Vikings were two-touchdown favorites. Their strong suit was defense. And their defensive front four had a special nickname which referred to the color of their jerseys. What were the Vike defenders called?

    The Purple People Eaters.

4. Kansas City got its first nine points from its Norwegian-born kicker, Jan Stenerud. Where did Jan attend college?

   Montana State. He went there on a skiing scholarship.

5. A short pass by Len Dawson was turned into a 46-yard touchdown by Kansas City's ace wide receiver. Name him.

   Otis Taylor. It was one of six catches he made during the game.

Super Bowl V, Miami
January 17, 1971

1. The first Super Bowl following the merger of the AFL and NFL matched two old NFL teams. Name them.

   The Dallas Cowboys (NFC) and Baltimore Colts (AFC).

2. Tom Landry, the Cowboys' original coach, led Dallas. Who coached Baltimore?

   First-year coach Don McCafferty. He took over when Don Shula left for Miami before the 1970 season.

3. As in most of the previous Super Bowls, the kickers played a major role. Dallas took a 6-0 lead on two field goals by whom?

   Mike Clark.

4. Dallas's quarterback started and went all the way. Name him.

   Craig Morton.

5. A 32-yard field goal with four seconds re-
    maining gave the Colts their 16-13 win.
    Who kicked it?

    Rookie Jim O'Brien.

Super Bowl VI, New Orleans
January 16, 1972

1. AFC champion Miami played in Super
    Bowl VI. How many years had the young
    Dolphins been in business?

    Six. The 1966 season was the team's first.

2. Cornerback Herb Adderley of Dallas
    completed his first Cowboy season in Su-
    per Bowl VI. How many Super Bowls
    had Herb played in before?

    **Two, with the Packers in the first two Su-
    per Bowls.**

3. Duane Thomas scored one of Dallas's
    three TDs. The two other Dallas six-
    pointers were scored by players who had
    started with other teams. Name them.

    **Mike Ditka, who first played with the
    Bears, and Lance Alworth, who starred
    with the Chargers.**

4. Miami's defensive unit gained great fame
    on the way to the AFC title. What nick-
    name were they known by?

    The No-Name Defense.

5. On its way to a 24-3 win, Dallas rolled up
    352 yards of offense. How many yards did
    Miami gain?

    185 — 105 passing and 80 rushing.

Super Bowl VII, Los Angeles
January 14, 1973

1. Miami made it two straight Super Bowl appearances in Super Bowl VII. Who were the Dolphins' opponents?

   George Allen's Old Men of Washington, the Redskins.

2. Bob Griese attempted only 11 passes in the game. How many did he complete?

   Eight for 88 yards (72.7%).

3. Who was the game's leading rusher?

   Miami's powerful Larry Csonka with 112 yards in 15 carries. Larry Brown led Washington with 72 yards.

4. Linebacker Chris Hanburger of Washington was an original Redskin draft choice. The other two linebackers came with coach Allen from Los Angeles. Name them.

   Myron Pottios and Jack Pardee.

5. Miami took a 14-0 lead in the first half. The 'Skins might have been shut out except for one glaring Dolphin mistake. What was it?

   On an attempted field goal, Miami kicker Garo Yepremian picked up a bad snap and tried to pass the ball. Washington's Mike Bass picked off the wobbly ball and returned it 49 yards for a score.

Super Bowl VIII, Houston
January 13, 1974

1. Miami tied Green Bay's record by winning its second straight Super Bowl. Who were the losers?

   The Minnesota Vikings, who also lost Super Bowl IV.

2. Marv Fleming, Miami's tight end, set a record for most Super Bowls played. How many?

   Five, two with Green Bay and three with Miami.

3. Larry Csonka scored two touchdowns, tying a Super Bowl record for TDs in a game. Which players share the mark?

   Max McGee of Green Bay (1967), Elijah Pitts of Green Bay (1967), and Bill Miller of Oakland (1968).

4. Garo Yepremian kicked a second-quarter field goal to give Miami a 17-0 lead. What was unique about it?

   It was the only field goal attempt of the game, another Super Bowl record.

5. Minnesota set a Super Bowl record for fewest punts returned with *none*. But, oddly, they don't hold the record for fewest yards on punt returns. How come?

   In Super Bowl VI, Dallas returned one punt for *minus one yard!*

Super Bowl IX, New Orleans
January 12, 1975

1. In this game of firsts, Pittsburgh won its first championship ever. Running back Franco Harris also established a first for the Steelers. In what category?

   Rushing. The Penn State grad became the first player ever to rush for more than 150 yards in a Super Bowl. His total? 159 yards.

2. Minnesota also established a first—one that the Vikes would like to forget. What was it?

   They became the first team to *lose* three Super Bowls.

3. Though originally scheduled for New Orleans' Superdome, the game had to be moved when the new stadium wasn't ready on time. Where was it played?

   Tulane Stadium, home of the Sugar Bowl.

4. Pittsburgh's victory was special for the Steeler quarterback who had lost his starting job earlier in the season. Name Pittsburgh's blond-bombshell QB.

   Terry Bradshaw.

5. Pittsburgh's front four pressured Minnesota's Fran Tarkenton all afternoon. And they accounted for another Super Bowl first. What did they do?

   They tackled Tarkenton for the first Super Bowl safety. That gave Pittsburgh a 2-0 halftime lead.